CREATING
the CONSTITUTION

1787

★ ★ *The Drama of* AMERICAN HISTORY ★ ★

CREATING
the CONSTITUTION

1787

Christopher Collier
James Lincoln Collier

BENCHMARK BOOKS

MARSHALL CAVENDISH
NEW YORK

ACKNOWLEDGMENT: The authors wish to thank Peter S. Onuf, Chair, Department of History, and Thomas Jefferson Memorial Foundation Professor, University of Virginia at Charlottesville, for his careful reading of the text of this volume of *Creating the Constitution* and his thoughtful and useful comments. This work has been much improved by Professor Onuf's notes. The authors are deeply in his debt, but of course, assume full responsibility for the substance of the work, including any errors that may appear.

Photo research by James Lincoln Collier

COVER PHOTO: © Independence National Historic Park

PICTURE CREDITS: The photographs in this book are used by permission and through the courtesy of: Independence National Historic Park: 10, 12, 15, 22 (bottom), 30, 33, 35, 42, 43, 44 (top), 44 (bottom), 50, 76, 86. Corbis-Bettman: 13, 22 (top), 24, 25, 40, 53, 54, 57, 59, 60, 63, 65, 69, 71 (left), 71 (right), 77, 80, 81. Colonial Williamsburg Foundation: 14, 31. Historic Williamsburg Foundation: 49.

Maps by Laszlo Kubinyi

Benchmark Books
Marshall Cavendish Corporation
99 White Plains Road
Tarrytown, New York 10591-9001

Library of Congress Cataloging-in-Publication Data

Collier, Christopher, date
Creating the Constitution, 1787
Christopher Collier and James Lincoln Collier.
p.   cm. —   (The drama of American history)
Includes bibliographical references and index.
Summary: Examines the events and personalities involved in creating the Constitution of the United States in 1787, a document which has been the foundation of American democracy for over 200 years.
ISBN 0-7614-0776-6 (lib. bdg.)
1. United States—Politics and government—1783–1789—Juvenile literature. 2. United States. Constitutional Convention (1787)—Juvenile literature. 3. Constitutional history—United States—Juvenile literature.
[1. United States. Constitutional Convention (1787) 2. Constitutional history—United States.
3. United States—Politics and government—1783–1789.]
I. Collier, James Lincoln, date II. Title.
III. Series: Collier, Christopher, date Drama of American history.
E303.C59   1999   342.73'029—DC21
970.00497—dc20   CIP

Printed in Italy

5 6 4

CONTENTS

PREFACE

Over many years of both teaching and writing for students at all levels, from grammar school to graduate school, it has been borne in on us that many, if not most, American history textbooks suffer from trying to include everything of any moment in the history of the nation. Students become lost in a swamp of factual information, and as a consequence lose track of how those facts fit together, and why they are significant and relevant to the world today.

In this series, our effort has been to strip the vast amount of available detail down to a central core. Our aim is to draw in bold strokes, providing enough information, but no more than is necessary, to bring out the basic themes of the American story, and what they mean to us now. We believe that it is surely more important for students to grasp the underlying concepts and ideas that emerge from the movement of history, than to memorize an array of facts and figures.

The difference between this series and many standard texts lies in what has been left out. We are convinced that students will better remember the important themes if they are not buried under a heap of names, dates, and places.

In this sense, our primary goal is what might be called citizenship education. We think it is critically important for America as a nation and Americans as individuals to understand the origins and workings of the public institutions which are central to American society. We have asked ourselves again and again what is most important for citizens of our democracy to know so they can most effectively make the system work for them and the nation. For this reason, we have focused on political and institutional history, leaving social and cultural history less well developed.

This series is divided into volumes that move chronologically through the American story. Each is built around a single topic, such as the pilgrims, the Constitutional Convention, or immigration. Each volume has been written so that it can stand alone, for students who wish to research a given topic. As a consequence, in many cases material from previous volumes is repeated, usually in abbreviated form, to set the topic in its historical context. That is to say, students of the Constitutional Convention must be given some idea of relations with England, and why the revolution was fought, even though the material was covered in detail in a previous volume. Readers should find that each volume tells an entire story that can be read with or without reference to other volumes.

Despite our belief that it is of the first importance to outline sharply basic concepts and generalizations, we have not neglected the great dramas of American history. The stories that will hold the attention of students are here, and we believe they will help the concepts they illustrate to stick in their minds. We think, for example, that knowing of Abraham Baldwin's brave and dramatic decision to vote with the small states at the Constitutional Convention will bring alive the Connecticut Compromise, out of which grew the American Senate.

Each of these volumes has been read by esteemed specialists in its particular topic; we have benefited from their comments.

CHAPTER I

The Articles of Confederation

It is, said William Gladstone, the celebrated nineteenth-century English politician, "the most remarkable work known to me in modern times to have been produced by the human intellect at a single stroke. . . ." Many historians agree with Gladstone. The American Constitution is certainly one of the most important documents written in modern times, and a case can be made that it is one of the most important pieces of writing ever.

Why can we make such bold claims for this work, which is only about a dozen pages—fewer than six thousand words? For one thing, it finally bound the very argumentative thirteen original states into a single republic, which would, a hundred and fifty years later, be the most powerful and influential nation on earth. Without the Constitution or something very much like it, there would be no United States of America as we know it, and the history of the world would have been much different.

For another, the liberties set forth in the Constitution and its first ten amendments, the Bill of Rights, exploded onto a world in which few people were truly free. The Declaration of Independence, adopted in 1776, inspired people everywhere to find freedom for themselves, and within a

This famous painting, by Thomas Rossiter, shows the Founding Fathers sign-
ing the Constitution in what is now called Independence Hall. Rossiter was
not, of course, painting from life, but drew upon his imagination to set the
stage. George Washington is seated at the desk at top.

generation, nations—especially in Latin America—began to overthrow
their colonial masters. The Constitution of 1787 provided all these new
nations, and those of the nineteenth and twentieth centuries as well, with
a model of how their freedoms could be secured. By what magic, then,
did this great document come into being?

It was no easy task. There were more forces pulling the states apart
than pushing them together. They were quite different from one another
in many ways. The New England states had a great shipbuilding industry and earned a lot of their money through fishing and trade. The

Southern states, by contrast, had few ships. They earned their money by growing tobacco, rice, and other crops, and depended upon New England ships to carry much of their produce to markets at home and abroad.

In the Southern states a large proportion of the labor was provided by slaves, and a whole way of life was built around slavery. The Northern states were gradually eliminating slavery; many people there, although by no means most, thought that slavery ought to be forbidden.

Religious ideas varied considerably. In the Southern states a tolerant Anglicanism—after 1784, Episcopalianism—dominated. In Pennsylvania the Quaker religion, with pacifist ideas, was strong. Maryland had been founded as a haven for Catholics, and New Englanders were imbued with the stern Calvinism of their Puritan forefathers.

The majority of Americans were descended from English men and women. Nonetheless, other nationalities were represented. New York had been founded by the Dutch, and the Dutch language was widely spoken there. There were pockets of Germans in Pennsylvania, French Huguenots in the Carolinas, Swedes in Delaware—all speaking their own languages. Some states had large populations of blacks, some of Indians, some of both. The states plainly had different needs and interests. Could they ever compromise those needs?

A second serious roadblock to unity was a deep-seated fear of power that was basic to American ways of thinking. Almost from the beginning, Americans had been trying to fend off the authority of their British rulers. Beginning more than a century before 1787 they had begun to see that their interests were often different from those of the British, and in the end Americans had to fight a great Revolution to rid themselves of British authority.

And then, suddenly, with the signing of the Declaration of Independence, the thirteen former colonies, now independent nations, or states, discovered that they had to form a government to replace the one they had rejected. The big problem was, how do you create a government that would have enough power to get necessary jobs done, without becoming tyrannical? It is very important, as we look at the era of the Constitutional Convention of 1787, to keep firmly in mind that the first loyalty of these early Americans had not been to the British Empire they were no longer a part of, nor to anything that might be called America. It was instead to their own states. These citizens of Pennsylvania, Rhode Island, Georgia, and the rest felt, as patriotic people do everywhere, that their own state was the best and ought not to have to change the way they did things just because some larger state thought they should. As the Revolution began, the majority of Americans had no intention of setting

The North depended on shipping and commerce for much of its wealth. This view of Philadelphia, painted around the time of the Constitutional Convention, shows a very busy port.

The South, by contrast, gained most of its wealth from growing crops like tobacco for sale to other states and foreign nations.

up a national government that might be as tyrannical as the British government had seemed to them. They wanted only just enough control at the top as was needed to get a few things done—mainly fight the Revolution.

Yet, as ever, opinion was divided. There were those who wanted a strong national government. Some people had made deals with Indians for large chunks of land in the territory north and west of the Ohio River, and they wanted a national government strong enough to uphold their claims. Others wanted a central government solid enough to pay its debts and to make sure that the states and private individuals paid their debts promptly, too. Still others wanted a government that could write trade laws binding on the states and make treaties with foreign nations, so that commerce would flow easily. Many wanted a strong national government simply because they thought it would get things done more effectively. But these were the minority, as quickly became clear when the states first tried to form a government.

George III of England symbolized for Americans the sort of tyrant they feared. They had freed themselves of George and England, and were determined never again to let anybody gain power over them. In writing the Constitution they were very careful about giving too much power to anybody.

That happened in 1774, when twelve of the states sent delegates to Philadelphia to discuss ways to deal with British efforts to tax them. (Readers interested in more detail on the events leading up to the Revolution can find them in the book of this series titled *The American Revolution*.) A second Continental Congress, as these meetings were called, met in 1775. While it was meeting, fighting broke out between British troops and Massachusetts militias in the famous battle of Lexington and Concord. The war was on, and in July 1776, when the Declaration of Independence made the rebellion official, the Continental Congress set about writing a constitution for the American government.

At first the strong nationalists held sway, but very quickly the old fear of putting too much power in one body flared up. The scheme of government embodied in this first national constitution, the Articles of Confederation, was a weak one. Indeed, it was not truly a government as

This drawing by Amos Doolittle shows British troops being attacked by minutemen from behind walls and trees as they cross the Concord Bridge.

we understand the term today, but a federation much like the modern United Nations. It was simply an organization of states put together to deal with common problems, mainly the war against the British. Under the Articles of Confederation there would be no powerful executive, no Supreme Court. The Congress would decide everything, down to the kind of uniforms army officers would wear and which sort of rifles would be bought for the troops.

A key principle was that in the Congress, each state, no matter how big or how populous, would have one vote. This was in line with the idea that the new government was merely a federation of equal states. At first the big states—Virginia, Pennsylvania, and Massachusetts—objected vociferously to this plan. They saw that under this scheme a few small states, with only a fraction of the American population, could control the Congress.

But the small states saw it the other way. If the vote was to be according to the population of each state, the "Big Three" with one or two allies could permanently dominate the government. There was so little agreement on this and other issues that nothing was decided; the Congress let it go and turned its mind to fighting the Revolution. The Articles of Confederation did not get through the Congress until 1777 and was not ratified by the states until 1781, when the Revolution was almost over.

Even before ratification, however, it was clear to at least some people that the proposed government would not be strong enough to do what was necessary. The Articles of Confederation said flatly that each state would keep "its sovereignty, freedom, and independence, and every power, jurisdiction and right" that was not explicitly turned over to the Continental Congress. The powers given up were not many. The Congress would have the authority to declare war and negotiate a peace, conduct foreign affairs, direct military operations, make a budget, and borrow money. But it lacked the power to force the states to do anything they didn't want to do. True, the Articles said that the states must "abide by the determinations" of Congress, but in practice states obeyed only such determinations as they chose to and ignored the others.

The effects of this lack of real power were felt throughout the war. Again and again George Washington and others trying to keep the battle going would beseech the states to send money, arms, troops, and provisions. Again and again the states sent part of what was asked for or none of it, as it suited them. Sometimes states took for themselves money they had raised for Washington. Many historians believe that Washington's greatest strength was his ability, over those long years of fighting, to cajole enough supplies from the states to keep up the fight.

The government under the Articles of Confederation was not a total failure. It carried on successful negotiations with France and Spain for support against the English and managed to borrow large amounts of money from foreign nations, as well as from Americans at home. In the end, the war was won.

Indeed, under the Continental Congresses of 1774 to 1781 and the Articles of Confederation from 1781 to 1789, the old Congress actually accomplished a great deal. Especially under the circumstances of fighting a war and carrying on diplomatic negotiations, with no power to tax and no ability to make anyone do anything, it is amazing how much got done.

For one thing, Congress did manage to finance the Revolution to a successful conclusion. These years also gave experience in national affairs, not only to the men who served in Congress but also to a cadre of treasury clerks, foreign diplomats, Indian agents, and other government functionaries.

Of very great importance in making possible the compromises and consensus at the Constitutional Convention of 1787 was the settlement of many conflicting land claims left over from the old colonial charters with their overlapping boundaries. Right up to the eve of the Convention, states were still contesting land claims. The last major controversy over

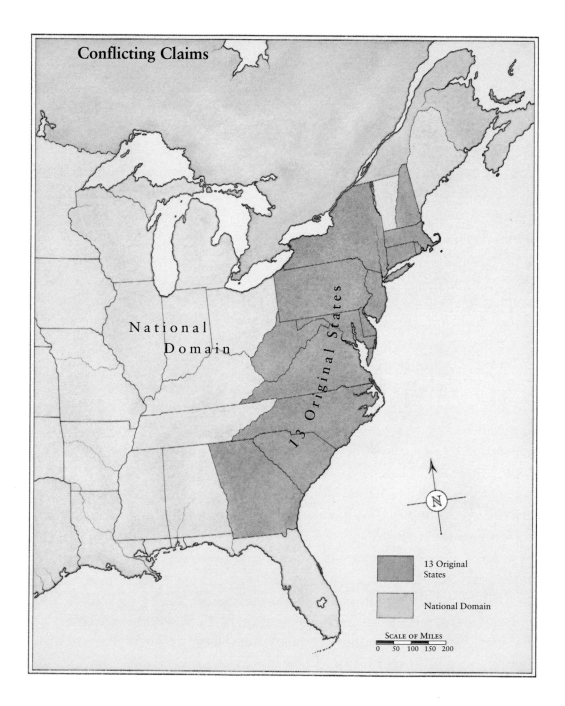

Conflicting Claims

National Domain

13 Original States

13 Original States

National Domain

SCALE OF MILES
0   50   100 150 200

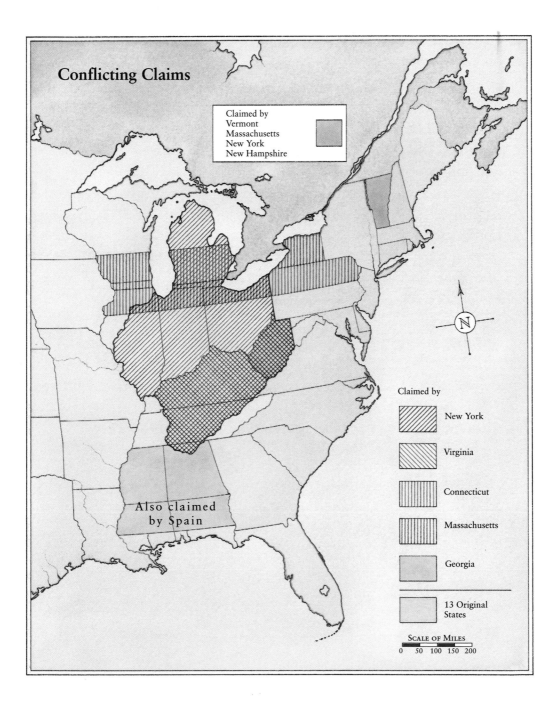

Conflicting Claims

Claimed by
Vermont
Massachusetts
New York
New Hampshire

Claimed by

New York

Virginia

Connecticut

Massachusetts

Georgia

13 Original
States

Also claimed
by Spain

N

SCALE OF MILES
0   50   100 150 200

land was finally settled in the only interstate court set up under the provisions of the Articles of Confederation, when in 1786 Pennsylvania's claim to territory in the Wyoming Valley, occupied by Connecticut settlers, was confirmed. By 1787, then, this most troublesome set of quarrels had been resolved; all the states had resigned their territorial claims north of the Ohio River to Congress. In the Northwest Ordinance of 1787 Congress organized this huge territory—today constituting five states and part of a sixth. At the time, Congress hoped to realize a tremendous income from its sale, though as it turned out, its hopes were too optimistic.

Thus, though the old Congress was unable to fulfill the needs of the newly independent states struggling to be a nation, it provided a platform—wobbly as it may have been—from which the new United States could be launched.

But even with these important accomplishments, by the end of the war it was clear to a great many people that the system was seriously flawed. Talk about improving it had gone on almost from the beginning. And then, in 1783, with the signing of the peace treaty that assured American independence, things began to go from bad to worse.

CHAPTER II

Danger Everywhere

The problems faced by the United States of America were formidable. One was that the British, French, and Spanish saw that the new nation was troubled and might soon fall apart. The Spanish were poised in Florida and across the Mississippi, the British were in Canada, the French in the Caribbean—and all waiting like wolves surrounding a flock of sheep, ready to pounce on the strays. The British had found an excuse to keep troops in bases around the Great Lakes, which violated the terms of the peace treaty. Many Americans still felt that they would be better off in the British Empire, and should the country encounter serious trouble, a lot of them would be ready to return to British control.

Then there were the Indians: The majority of them had sided with the British during the Revolution, and feelings between them and whites were very bad. Most of the whites now felt that America was theirs and had no compunction about pushing into Indian territory to carve out farms. There was open warfare, with both sides occasionally massacring women and children. Some of the settlers on the western frontier were ready to ally themselves with the Spanish across the Mississippi for help

(above) Many European nations felt that the squabbling former colonies would soon fall into disunity and would be easy prey. This cartoon shows England, which had lost a leg in the Revolution, trying to tug the colonies back under its control.

(left) Joseph Brant, one of the greatest Indian chiefs in the eastern part of the continent, fought with the British during the Revolution, and remained a constant threat to American settlers on the frontier across the Appalachian Mountains.

against the Indians. If that happened, Spain might well take over huge pieces of the western lands. Already, the Spanish were insisting that the Mississippi River was theirs.

A more distant but significant enemy were the Barbary pirates operating in the Mediterranean off the north coast of Africa. They were capturing American ships, enslaving passengers and crews, and stealing cargoes. Something clearly had to be done about the Barbary pirates.

Another very serious problem was the fact that with the Revolution, the British closed their ports to American ships. Americans had for a hundred and fifty years done an enormous amount of business with such British islands as Jamaica and the Bahamas, as well as with England itself. Now this business was closed off; somehow, the British West Indian ports had to be opened up again.

Again, during the war, the Continental Congress had borrowed huge amounts of money from foreign investors, foreign nations, and tens of thousands of ordinary Americans who had been given IOUs instead of money for service or supplies given the army. The states too had borrowed money for the war and other purposes. Many people thought that the national government should pay off these state debts; but how could Congress pay state debts when it could not pay its own? Clearly, if the United States was to have any credit with the world, the debts would have to be paid.

Solutions could be found to all these problems. The huge debt could be paid off over time, provided that each state put some money into the national pot. The British could be pushed out of their Great Lakes forts by a determined show of force. Treaties could be negotiated with Spain for use of the Mississippi, if the states could agree on what to do with the wilderness territory to the west. The answers were not hard to find, but they could be made to work only if the states were willing to make some sacrifices for the good of the whole nation.

The problem was that they were not. For example, in 1785

Finding money to buy clothes, food, and equipment for his troops during the Revolution was a constant problem for Washington. The terrible winter at Valley Forge in Pennsylvania, when the troops lived on corn bread much of the time and many went barefoot, has become an American legend. This artist's recreation shows a soldier in rags shivering in the snow.

Massachusetts, Rhode Island, and New Hampshire saw that if they barred British merchant ships from their ports, they might be able to force them to open up British West Indian ports in exchange. These three states passed laws to do this, but Connecticut, hoping to gather the British trade to itself, refused to go along and the plan collapsed.

Another constant source of conflict were state borders. The original colonies had been laid out rather haphazardly by people in London who had little idea of American geography, and many states had overlapping claims. Connecticut and Pennsylvania actually fought a brief war over what is now a portion of Pennsylvania. States would have to compromise on these borders.

Again, despite the fact that in the peace treaty with England Congress had to agree to return land and slaves taken from Loyalists during the war, the state of Virginia passed laws refusing to do this. Georgia and North Carolina ignored treaties made with the Indians by the Congress under the Articles, and made treaties of their own. And none of the states was eager to raise money from its citizens for the Confederation.

It was becoming clearer and clearer to farseeing people that unless something was done, the nation was likely to fall apart before it had hardly begun. Governor John Hancock of Massachusetts told his legislature, "How to strengthen and improve the Union so as to render it completely adequate, demands the immediate attention of the states." James Madison wrote to James Monroe, both of whom would later be president, "If the present paroxysm of our affairs be totally neglected, our case may become desperate."

John Hancock was one of the most powerful politicians in Massachusetts, and the state's governor for nine terms. Shays' Rebellion took place in his state, and it is not surprising that he was much alarmed by the weakness of the national government.

As it happened, about this time Madison was involved with meetings among various states to thrash out some commercial matters. The idea came up of calling a conference of all the states, and Madison and some others, including George Washington, seized on it as a chance to revise the Articles of Confederation. A call went out for a meeting to be held in Philadelphia on the second Monday in May 1787. In the months leading up to May, Madison and his allies caucused, canvassed, wrote letters, argued. In the end, all state legislatures except Rhode Island's voted to send delegations to Philadelphia. And then occurred an event that did more than anything else to open the eyes of people to the inadequacies of the American government.

It sounds strange today, but at that time the United States had no money of its own. People used foreign coins, such as Dutch guilders, French livres, Spanish doubloons, and particularly English shillings, to do business. For a variety of complicated reasons, hard money was in short supply in the United States. That was not always a problem, for most ordinary people used a barter system, trading with a shopkeeper a barrel of cider or bushel of wheat for the needles, shovels, and glassware they needed.

But many taxes had to be paid in real money. By the mid-1780s many farmers were having trouble finding the money to pay their taxes. They fell behind, and then sheriffs would arrive at the farms to auction off tools, an ox, perhaps the whole farm.

The loss of even an ox was a terrible thing for a farmer, who would now be unable to plow his fields. Farmers demanded from their legislatures "stay" laws, which would postpone all debts for a year or so. They demanded that the state issue paper money. In those days people mistrusted paper money and insisted on metal coins—gold, silver, copper—called *specie*. People who were owed money often refused to take paper money, so the debtors demanded that legislatures pass "tender" laws, requiring creditors to accept paper money in payment of debts.

But even these laws did not solve the problems of farm people, and they turned to illegal methods. They banded together to stop sheriffs' auctions. Sometimes they burned down courthouses to destroy records of their cases.

Matters were particularly bad in Massachusetts. There the government had decided to tax people heavily to pay off the state's war debt. Paying off the debt was a good idea, but taxing people for money they did not have was not. The government, controlled by wealthy men from the seacoast, seemed not to understand the terrible hardship they were imposing on the farmers. All around the state, but especially at the western end of it, farmers went about closing courts and stopping tax auctions. Very quickly this resistance turned into an organized movement—a rebellion, in fact. These farmers had just fought and won a rebellion against the mighty British. Could they not fight another one against the tyrants—as they saw them—in Boston?

Leadership of this rebellion fell upon Daniel Shays, a hero of the Revolution who had fought at Bunker Hill. The Massachusetts government dithered, then finally put together an army that marched out to deal with the rebels. Shays decided to capture an arsenal in Springfield. The government called out the Massachusetts militia—what we would today call the National Guard. The militia was made up of ordinary farmers very much like the rebels of Shays' army who were marching against them. Would the militia fire on people like themselves?

The arsenal was at the top of a hill. On a snowy winter day Shays' little army began to toil up it. The militiamen fired some cannons into them. Four people were killed, and Shays' army broke and ran. Eventually a number of Shays' rebels were jailed and sentenced to death, although in the end they were pardoned. Daniel Shays went into hiding in New York state.

Shays' Rebellion had not been very well organized and had been put down fairly easily. But that it had occurred at all was very disturbing to thoughtful people. Even more disturbing was the fact that the national government had had no power to end it or to put a stop to the courthouse burnings occurring in other states. The need for a stronger national government seemed increasingly clear to many people after Shays' Rebellion.

Indeed, to many influential men from New Hampshire to Georgia, it looked as if the loosely joined states might fly apart and reestablish themselves as three or four little regional unions at odds with each other, individually prey to reconquest by the British or to domination by Spain or France. On the other hand, there was much talk of setting up a kind of a king and restoring order through a military government of some sort. If George Washington had not been so determinedly opposed to such a plan, but had instead lent himself to it, a new monarchy would have been a very real possibility.

The fears were real, and Shays' Rebellion gave them substance, coming as it did just after the call for a convention. Thus the appeal to try again to construct a new, workable government for the United States was taken seriously by America's leading figures.

CHAPTER III

The Great Men Gather

Twelve states responded affirmatively to the call to Philadelphia. In all, seventy-seven men were chosen to go, but only fifty-five actually attended. They gathered slowly in early May 1787. It was a more leisurely time, when travel was not easy. They were not all there on that Monday, May 14. It rained hard all day, and one man who lived close by did not come. He was Benjamin Franklin, aged and ill, and he would wait for better weather. But it was clear that it would be a gathering of "demi-gods," as Thomas Jefferson, who was representing the American government in Paris, put it. The genius Franklin and Washington, the military hero, enjoyed international reputations: Washington had managed to beat the mighty British army against all odds, and Franklin had made important contributions to science and literature.

Not far behind them were clear-thinking men such as James Madison, Roger Sherman of Connecticut, James Wilson of Pennsylvania, Charles Pinckney of South Carolina, and Gouverneur Morris of New York, who would play major roles in shaping the government-to-be. Others—William Paterson of New Jersey, John Dickinson of Pennsylvania,

29

Next to Washington, Benjamin Franklin was the most revered of Americans, famous not only at home but in Europe as well, where he had spent many years as America's representative to both England and France. Not only a fine writer and brilliant diplomat, he had also made important discoveries about the nature of electricity. By 1787 his influence was waning, but his wisdom continued to be valued.

William S. Johnson of Connecticut, for example—would have shone in any company less brilliant than this.

These were not typical Americans. There were few small farmers—a category that formed the bulk of Americans—among them. They were all white males, all but one Protestant. More than half were lawyers, many were wealthy, and all had held public office before as state legislators, governors, or judges. A large proportion had served in the Continental Congresses and in Congress under the Articles of Confederation. Indeed, sixteen of the Convention delegates were at the same time members of Congress. Thirty had fought in the revolution, eight had signed the Declaration of Independence. Among them were a few men of no particular brilliance and one or two outright scoundrels. But in the main, these were the "stars" of America. It was as if today we called together all the best and brightest Americans to discuss the country's ills.

Many of these people were intellectuals who had studied political questions carefully. But more importantly, they were all practical politi-

A typical delegate to the Constitutional Convention was George Wythe of Virginia, a judge and professor of law at William and Mary College. This picture shows Wythe's dining room as it was at the time of the Convention. Wythe, obviously, was no simple farmer, but a man of wealth and learning.

cians with wide experience in government. They were conservative almost by nature. They were not out to overthrow the system, but to make it work better. While they believed that in the eyes of God all men are created equal, they also believed that on earth they are not: some would lead and some would follow, some would be wealthy, some scratch hard livings from the soil. A good many of them even believed that some people were bound to be masters, some slaves.

Their meeting place was the brick building known today as Independence Hall, a commodious place two stories high topped by a cupola and a spire. Most of the time they met in the east room, forty-by-forty feet, the size of a large classroom. The delegates sat in threes and fours at tables covered with a soft green fabric.

They began by electing George Washington president of the Convention. That was automatic: so admired was Washington that no other choice could be thought of. Today we have trouble understanding why Washington was so revered in his time. We know him mostly from the stiff, grim-faced portraits of him in his general's uniform. We cannot imagine him smiling, much less laughing. His close friends knew a different Washington—a warmhearted, generous man, one of the finest horsemen of his day, fearless in battle, a man who enjoyed hunting or staying up late to dance and play cards. Yet as high-spirited as he was, he loved his country and would sacrifice himself for it on the battlefield, at the Constitutional Convention, and as president.

Washington would speak rarely during the meeting, although he was influential behind the scenes. The leading role at the Convention was played by James Madison. Indeed, historians today sometimes call him The Father of the Constitution. Not only did Madison play an important part in the debates, speaking many times each day, but he brought into the Convention a carefully worked-out scheme of government, much of which ended up in the finished document.

Madison, the son of a wealthy planter, had been educated at

James Madison was one of the most important Americans who ever lived. His ideas were vastly influential at the Convention, he became the fourth president, and was a political power in America for some sixty years.

Princeton, where he completed the three-year course in two years and then went on to study religion. He was a rather shy young man. Once, when he was staying at an inn in Williamsburg, somebody reached through an open window and stole his hat. In those days men were expected to wear hats in public; Madison was so embarrassed by the thought of going out without his hat that he stayed inside until he could get another one. He was, according to one man, "a gentleman of great modesty—with a remarkable sweet temper," who was "easy and unreserved among his acquaintances."

However personally shy, Madison was intellectually bold. He had been active in the Virginia legislature and was also in the Continental Congress. Madison was particularly disturbed by the states' stay and tender laws, which seemed to him legalized robbery of money fairly owed, but he was also aware of the other problems the United States was running into. In 1786 he sat down to make a deliberate study of political history. He then wrote a paper on what he saw to be the flaws in the government under the Articles of Confederation. According to one historian,

Madison's "chief concern was the unrestricted power of majorities in state legislatures to pass laws that violated the rights of individuals and minorities. Thus the great task of reform was to strengthen the national government *and* provide justice for individuals."

Madison was intensely concerned about power. He wanted a national government strong enough to put down rebellions and prevent state legislatures from rewriting the laws with every passing political change but one that would not have so much power that it might interfere with people's basic rights.

Immediately as the Convention opened, Madison chose a seat for himself where he could see and hear everything that went on. Every day he took careful notes on what was said, and every evening, instead of relaxing in his lodging as most delegates did, he would go to his room and copy over his notes while they were fresh in his mind. Madison's "Notes," as historians call them, are the best source we have for what was said in Independence Hall during that long Philadelphia summer. Other delegates also took notes, but they are fragmentary. Though there was an official secretary to record the votes, that's about all he recorded, so it is Madison's Notes that we count on.

Finally, the Convention voted to impose secrecy on itself. There would be no press briefings, no daily reports in the newspapers about the debates. This was a critically important decision, for it allowed the delegates to speak frankly, to float unpopular ideas, to change their positions on issues, without people looking over their shoulders all the time. The delegates took the rule of secrecy seriously; nothing leaked out. Once, somebody found on the floor outside the meeting room a copy of a paper that had been distributed to the delegates. It was brought to Washington. He sternly admonished the delegates to be more careful. He said, "I know not whose paper it is, but here it is, let him who owns it take it." He flung the paper down on his table and stalked out of the room, leaving the delegates cowed. Needless to say, nobody claimed the lost paper.

William Jackson, shown here, was the official recorder at the Convention, but he noted only the results of the votes. Historians rely on Madison's lengthy notes, which are our primary record of what happened at the Convention.

The preliminaries out of the way, the Convention got down to business. That business took a tortuous path. Following the debates is not easy. Matters were raised, discussed, dropped, raised again, dropped again. Issues were settled and then unsettled. Some items that came up in the first days were still being argued over at the end. Everything was intermeshed: Change one matter here, and half a dozen seemingly unrelated points would have to be changed, too.

To give one example of how everything was tied together, some delegates believed that the president ought to serve for only one term so he could not become entrenched in power. If he were to serve for only one term, it ought to be a long one, to give the government some stability. But if the term was long, it should be possible to impeach him if he were to commit a crime. On the other hand, if the president could be reelected, he could have a short term, and there would be no need for impeachment because he would soon be coming up for reelection anyway. At the Convention everything depended on everything else.

In order to simplify the story, we will look at only a few major conflicts that had to be settled if the country was to get a new Constitution. Then we will look at the basic principles of the Constitution that grew out of the debates during that summer. Understanding the Constitution is of critical importance for all Americans, for it is this brief document that protects our liberties and, by keeping our nation from falling into chaos, allows us to get on with our lives. Nothing matters so much as this.

CHAPTER IV

Compromises

One of the issues to beset the Convention almost from the moment it began was the conflict between the more populous states and the smaller ones. Virginia, Pennsylvania, and Massachusetts combined had almost half the population of the United States; each was more than ten times larger than small states such as Delaware, New Jersey, and Rhode Island.

Today it is difficult to understand what the fuss was all about. People from Rhode Island and Delaware rarely find themselves allied on some issue against New York and California. States are more likely to ally themselves around common interests—the industrial Northeast against the agricultural West, the Sun Belt against the Snow Belt.

We remember, however, that Americans felt deeply loyal to their own states. The small states were determined not to allow the big states to dominate them. They had insisted that under the Articles of Confederation each state would have an equal vote, and the same rule was in effect at the Convention itself because Madison and other big-state men knew that the small states would not have sent delegations to Philadelphia otherwise.

There was another element to it, however. The United States under the Articles of Confederation was a *federation*—a group of independent states joined for certain purposes. The idea of a federation itself at least suggested all the members were equal and should have equal votes.

To James Madison and his big-state allies, this was absurd. Why should tiny Rhode Island have the same vote as Pennsylvania, with ten times Rhode Island's population? The scheme of government that Madison brought to the Convention, known as the Virginia Plan, called for delegations to Congress to be based on population—proportional representation, as it is called. Anything else would be grossly unfair, in Madison's view.

Once again, there was a second idea involved. Madison believed that governments ought to be built on the will of the people. We will look at this idea in more detail later. This meant that the new government must not be constructed by the states, but must be authorized by the people and must operate directly on them. For example, under the Articles of Confederation, the national government could not tax people directly, as we do today, but must ask for money from the states, which could raise it however they wanted. If the government were to be based on the people, each citizen must have the same power, which meant that the vote in Congress should be by population.

Madison assumed that the least populated states would bow to the logic of this. But those states had no intention of bowing to the big states on anything. Almost immediately Delaware threatened to walk out if the big states insisted on proportional representation.

The trouble was that the big states had the votes. The delegates from New Hampshire, a small state, had not yet come, because of wrangling at home, and would be long in coming; Rhode Island never sent a delegation at all. There were only three big states, but it was generally believed by everybody at the Convention that the three southernmost states—Georgia and the Carolinas—would quickly grow in population.

They all had large areas of empty land that would soon fill up and give them large populations, too. That gave the big states six votes, a majority of one. Very quickly, the big states shoved through the Virginia Plan, with its proportional representation in Congress.

Everyone knew that this would not be accepted by the small states, and for the moment the issue was dropped. Why? The delegates were increasingly coming to feel that the Convention could not, must not, fail to produce a new, workable government for the United States. If they returned to the old system, the country would split up, and the French, Spanish, and English would pounce and swallow up the states one by one. Some of the big-states' delegates believed that the big states could confederate on their own and the others would be forced to come in. But most delegates believed it had to be all the states or none, and they were determined to find compromises.

Then, on June 9, William Paterson of New Jersey forced the issue. He pointed out that the Convention had not been authorized to alter the Articles of Confederation so drastically as to abandon equal voting. The people were not prepared for anything so radical and would not support it, he said.

In response, James Wilson of Pennsylvania retorted, "Are not the citizens of Pennsylvania equal to those of New Jersey? Does it require one hundred fifty of the former to balance fifty of the latter? . . . If the small states will not confederate on [the principle of proportional representation,] Pennsylvania and . . . some other states would not confederate on any other."

Paterson knew he could not win on a showdown vote, and the small states would then be forced to accept proportional representation or leave. He moved to postpone the vote until the next session. The relieved delegates agreed.

Luckily, the next day was Sunday, when there would be no meeting. It now appears that Paterson used Sunday to meet with other small-state men to work out a plan of action. Among these people was Roger Sherman of Connecticut. His name does not ring in the ears with the resonance of Washington, Franklin, or Madison. Yet Roger Sherman was one of the half-dozen most important men at the Convention—indeed, one of the most important politicians in America. He signed the Declaration and Resolves of 1774 that led to the confrontation with England. He was on the committee appointed to write the Declaration of Independence, and he signed it. He was on the committee that wrote the Articles of Confederation and spent more time in the Confederation Congress than any other man. He was, according to Thomas Jefferson, "a man who never said a foolish thing in his life." He was not a great speaker and, being the sort of man who was never foolish, did not become the subject of stories and legends. But at the Constitutional Convention he was a key figure.

Back in 1776, when Sherman was helping to write the

Roger Sherman is today far less renowned than some of the other men at the Constitutional Convention, like James Madison and Benjamin Franklin, but he was one of the most important of the Founding Fathers, responsible for inventing the Connecticut Compromise, which saved the Convention and established our bicameral Congress.

old Articles of Confederation, he recognized the inevitable conflict between big and small states over how Congress should vote—by population or by state. Sherman's own Connecticut was actually middle-sized, but it tended to side with the small states. Sherman looked for a compromise and came up with a novel solution: Vote on every issue twice, once with every state equal and once by population. Only proposals that passed both tallies would become law. In 1776, however, the idea was too unusual and was dropped.

But as everybody knew, the British government had a two-house—bicameral—Parliament, with a House of Commons and a House of Lords. All the states but Pennsylvania also had bicameral legislatures. Madison had proposed one in his Virginia Plan. Now, on that crucial Monday in Philadelphia, Roger Sherman proposed what has become known as the Connecticut Compromise—Madison's bicameral legislature, but with one house based on proportional representation and the other house having one vote per state. But the big states held firm. They wanted proportional representation in both houses.

Still, nobody walked out. Once again the Convention turned to other matters. But the issue could not be put off indefinitely. The small states began to realize that their only hope was the Connecticut Compromise. By June the arguing was bitter. James Wilson of Pennsylvania cried, "Can we forget for whom we are forming a government? Is it for men, or for imaginary beings called states?" Gunning Bedford, a tempestuous delegate from little Delaware, shouted to the big-states men, "I do not, gentlemen, trust you. . . . Sooner than be ruined, there are foreign powers who will take us by the hand." It was almost a call for civil war.

Fortunately once again, the next day was Sunday. Many of the delegates were in despair. Gouverneur Morris of New York dropped in at the home of his friend Robert Morris, where George Washington was staying. He found the two men "much dejected . . . and at this alarming crisis, a dissolution of the Convention was hourly to be expected."

The fight between the big and small states appeared for a time to be insoluble. Gouverneur Morris, a delegate from New York who favored strong government, reported that Washington was in despair over the situation.

But over that weekend a seemingly small thing happened that would have large consequences for the history of the world. Three delegates, two from Georgia and one from North Carolina, left Philadelphia. They were also members of the old Congress under the Articles of Confederation, which was still meeting in New York. Some matters of importance to their states were coming up in Congress, and as it looked as if the Convention was going to break up anyway, they decided it was more important to be in Congress. They were, as it turned out, very wrong about that.

On Monday morning the Convention began the critical vote on the Connecticut Compromise. The order of voting was north to south. As the New Hampshire delegation still had not arrived, Massachusetts voted first. As expected, it voted no; it wanted proportional representation in both houses of Congress. Connecticut, New York—which at the time had about the same population as Connecticut or North Carolina—and New Jersey voted yes, in favor of the Connecticut Compromise calling for equal voting in one house. The big state Pennsylvania voted no; the small state Delaware voted yes.

Now it was Maryland's turn. The Maryland delegation consisted of two men. One was Luther Martin, a violently strong supporter of the small-state position. He would, of course, vote for the Connecticut Compromise. The other delegate, with the strange name of Daniel of Saint Thomas Jenifer, was a different sort. He was an old friend of George Washington's, and firmly in favor of a government based on the people. He frequently voted with the big states, canceling Luther Martin's vote. At this critical moment Jenifer was not in Independence Hall. Thus Luther Martin stood alone in the Maryland delegation, and he voted his state for the Connecticut Compromise.

Why was Jenifer absent at so important a moment? In fact, as soon as the vote was over he calmly strode into the hall. We can only conclude that he understood that the small states must

Luther Martin was a passionate defender of the interests of the small states. Daniel of Saint Thomas Jenifer deliberately stayed away from the crucial vote on the Connecticut Compromise to allow Martin to vote Maryland with the small states.

(left) Independence Hall in Philadelphia as it looks today. It has been changed over time, but in the eighteenth century it was much as it appears here.

(below) The Assembly Room where most of the meetings of the Convention were held. The delegates sat in groups of three or four at the green baize tables. George Washington, as president of the Convention, sat in the high chair at the table in the rear on a slightly raised platform.

have their way on this issue if the Convention were to succeed, and he stayed away deliberately to let Luther Martin vote Maryland for the Connecticut Compromise.

Clearly, the vote was going to be closer than the delegates had thought. The small states now had five votes, and when the big state Virginia voted against the Connecticut Compromise, the big states had three, with the three southernmost states expected to vote with them. North Carolina voted no, as expected; so did South Carolina. The score was now five to five. It was up to Georgia to cast the last, and deciding, vote.

Georgia had sent four delegates to the Convention. We remember, however, that two of them had gone to New York City. One of those remaining was William Houston, a firm supporter of the big-state position. The other was Abraham Baldwin. Baldwin had grown up in Connecticut, the son of a blacksmith. His mother had died when he was young. He had struggled to get an education at Yale, where he had been a brilliant student, and had become a lawyer. Only four years before the Convention met, he had moved to Georgia, where there were fewer lawyers than in Connecticut and better opportunities for him.

Baldwin knew the Connecticut people well, and there can be no doubt that Roger Sherman met with him from time to time as the Convention went on. Baldwin knew better than most of the big-state men that the small-staters would walk out if they did not get equal voting in at least one house of Congress, as the Connecticut Compromise called for. He also knew that Georgia, with the Spanish on its flank to the south and Indians on its back to the west, would be in serious trouble without the support of a strong United States. We can imagine the sort of pressure he must have felt on that critical Monday, what things must have stirred round and round in his mind. But Abraham Baldwin was a man of courage, one of those many men at the Convention who would rise above self-interest and do what was best for all. He voted with the small states for the Connecticut Compromise, canceling out Houston and

The critical vote on the Connecticut Compromise was cast by Abraham Baldwin of Georgia in an act of wisdom and courage.

dividing Georgia's vote, thus leaving the final tally five in favor of equal representation in one house, and five against.

The stunned Convention now realized that the small states would have equal voting in one house of Congress—the Senate, as it would be called. True, the vote was a tie, five to five, but the big-states men now saw what they might have seen earlier, that the small states had to have the Connecticut Compromise. One after another, delegates from the big states rose and announced, in effect, that they would accept it. James Madison of Virginia and James Wilson of Pennsylvania continued to fight a rear-guard action, but they were beaten. The Convention was saved.

Almost from the moment the Connecticut Compromise solved the conflict between big states and small, several things became clear: One was that some of the small-states delegates, which had previously been leery of a powerful government that might be dominated by the big states, reversed course. They believed it was best for them to have a strong national government that could curb the power of the big states. For example, New Jersey had no major seaport of its own. Goods moving

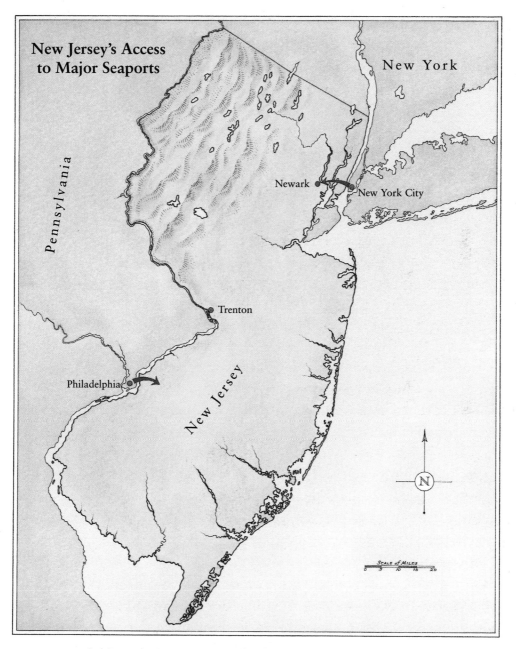

New Jersey's Access to Major Seaports

Pennsylvania

New York

Newark

New York City

Trenton

Philadelphia

New Jersey

N

SCALE OF MILES
0   5   10   15   20

New Jersey had no major seaport of its own, and used New York City and Philadelphia for its exports and imports. Needless to say, New Jerseyans resented paying import taxes to those cities, and hoped that a strong, new government would take over these taxes for the benefit of all the states.

in and out of the state were shipped mainly through New York or Philadelphia, where they could be taxed for the benefit of Pennsylvania and New York state. The small-states people saw that if the national government took over export and import taxes, the money would be used for the good of everybody, not just the states with good seaports.

This change of heart by some small-states men considerably strengthened the hand of delegates such as Madison, Washington, and Wilson, who wanted a strong national government.

A second fact to emerge after the passage of the Connecticut Compromise was that the real division at the Convention was between the northern and southern states, as James Madison had seen all along. These two regions of the country were different an many ways. Differences in climate and topography made for different lifestyles, different ways of earning livings. Southerners specialized in growing crops like rice, tobacco, and sugar on a large scale and selling them to both other colonies and other nations.

The northern states also exported large quantities of cash crops— wheat from Pennsylvania, codfish from Massachusetts, beef and pork from Connecticut—but in addition they depended on shipping and trade for much of their income. New Englanders in particular were great shipbuilders and seafarers, and their ships and traders were essential in carrying southern crops to market. Thus, northerners and southerners were often on opposite sides of business deals.

Moreover, many northerners adhered to Calvinist and Quaker ideals, which emphasized hard work and good deeds; in the South the chief religion was a more easygoing Anglicanism. Finally, and perhaps more crucially, the South had tens of thousands of slaves and the North had relatively few. Not all northerners were opposed to slavery; the Connecticut delegate William Samuel Johnson, for example, owned slaves. Many northerners, however, were opposed to slavery for religious and moral, as well as other, reasons.

But just as it had become clear that the small states would not confederate without some protection from the big ones, it was also clear that the southern states would not join the union if slavery was threatened.

The series of compromises that settled the North-South conflict is so complex and intermeshed with other issues that even experts have trouble following its crooked course. The key point is that the northern delegates used the lever of slavery to pry certain concessions from the South. The northerners knew that they could not go back to their people with a Constitution that left the importation of Africans untouched; back home

This picture showing slaves as "Virginian luxuries" represented the attitude of many northerners who disliked the whole idea of slavery and the way slaves were treated in the South.

Northerners were by no means all opposed to slavery. William Samuel Johnson, of Connecticut, a delegate to the convention and a major figure in his state, owned some slaves.

there was too much opposition to the foreign slave trade for that. The southern delegates understood this and knew they would have to give some ground.

But the northern delegates also knew that they could not push the southerners too hard on slavery, and it became their policy to use slavery as a bargaining chip on other issues, mainly economic ones that affected northern pocketbooks. When the dust settled, the bargaining between northern and southern delegates came down to this:

1. The importation of slaves would be permitted for at least twenty years. After 1808 Congress could abolish the importation of slaves if it wanted to. It was assumed that the population of the South would have grown to the point where it would control the House of Representatives, and therefore the slave trade would not be abolished. In fact, the southern population did not grow as expected, and the

South never controlled the House. In 1808 the Congress forbade the importation of any more slaves.

2. Export duties—that is, taxes on goods shipped out of American ports—would be forbidden by the new Constitution. The southerners were great exporters of tobacco, rice, and sugar, and hated export taxes. Some northern shippers did not like them either, but others felt these taxes would be a good way to raise money for the new nation. In the compromise, export taxes were forbidden.

3. Southern slave owners would be allowed to go into northern states in search of runaway slaves. In fact, it was difficult in practice for slave owners to ferret out runaways. Unfortunately, the law would be used by manhunters to kidnap free blacks in the North and take them south into slavery. This would always be a sore point with northerners who opposed slavery on principle.

4. Slavery would not be permitted in the so-called Northwest Territory—today the states of Ohio, Indiana, Illinois, Michigan, Wisconsin, and part of Minnesota.

The bargaining between the northern and southern delegates went right through to the end of the Constitutional Convention. But it gradually became clear that an agreement would somehow be reached. Now the delegates were able to concentrate on the basic issue that had brought them to Philadelphia in the first place: Which powers ought to be given to the national government, and which left to the states?

CHAPTER V

Principles

Under the Articles of Confederation, the states were their own masters and could ignore orders from the national government if they chose. This system had not worked, and most of the delegates came to Philadelphia feeling that the national government had to be strengthened. The question was, how much?

Some, like Roger Sherman, believed that the people of his state as a rule knew what was best for them; the national government should be given only such power as was absolutely necessary. Others, like James Wilson, wanted to leave the states virtually powerless. Probably most of the delegates were somewhere in the middle. Deciding where power should lie had to be worked out in terms of specific, practical questions such as: Who would control the army? Who would appoint ambassadors? How would the president be elected? It is not as important for us, however, to understand how the details were arrived at as it is to understand the basic principles behind the Constitution, so we can see not merely *how* it works, but *why* it works as it does.

Many of these principles were not fully understood by the delegates on that rainy Monday when the Convention opened. But through the endless debating and talking things through in evening conversations, the delegates did a lot of hard thinking about the nature of government—what it is and what it is supposed to do—and gradually the outlines of certain principles began to emerge. Let us look at them.

❧ The Idea of Natural Rights

Most of the delegates came to Philadelphia believing that all human beings possessed certain natural rights, as it says right at the beginning of the Declaration of Independence: people are "endowed by their Creator with certain unalienable Rights, that among these, are Life, Liberty, and the pursuit of Happiness." This idea of natural rights was much talked about during the time of the Revolution. You couldn't "prove" that people had natural or "unalienable" rights (*unalienable* means that they can't be taken away); it just seemed reasonable to the delegates that such rights existed.

Exactly what those rights were was another question. The delegates believed, for example, that people had a natural right to keep whatever they owned—money, land, furniture, any-

A page from the first draft of the Virginia Bill of Rights, which calls itself "A Declaration of Rights." Natural rights, in the view of many Americans of the day, did not have to be "proven" but were "self-evident" and could simply be declared.

Britain's Magna Carta, or Great Charter, was one of the first steps in limiting the freedom of kings to do as they liked to their people. It was a sort of contract between King John and his barons. In 1976, during the bicentennial of the Declaration of Independence, the oldest surviving copy of the Magna Carta, dated 1215, was loaned to the United States to show how American independence traced its roots way back into English history. The Magna Carta is part of the jumble of law and tradition that makes up the British "constitution."

thing. But what about cases in which a government needed to take over some farmland in order to put in a road? Spelling out the details of natural rights was not always easy, as we shall see when we discuss the Bill of Rights. Nevertheless, the delegates were sure that natural rights existed, and they put limits around what governments could do. A government, for example, could not simply take away people's land for a road, but had to show in court that it had good reasons for doing so—that taking from one would help the many. This concept of individual natural rights that put limits on government is a critical aspect of our Constitution.

◄ *The Social Contract*

Another idea that had been discussed by philosophers as far back as the Classical Era more than a century and a half earlier was the social contract. Various thinkers had different ideas about what the social contract consisted of. The theory of social contract most familiar to the delegates was the one described by John Locke, whose works appeared about a hundred years before the Convention and who was considered one of the great thinkers of his age.

According to Locke, the "prince"—meaning the ruler—had entered into an unwritten contract, or agreement, with the people he ruled. Under this contract the prince and the people each possessed certain rights and duties; generally speaking, the people owed the prince obedience, while the prince was required to look after the interests of the people he ruled. Of course, this was all theoretical. In practice, as any student of American history knows, kings often tried to run roughshod over their people. The American Revolution was fought in considerable part because Americans believed that George III was doing just that. Locke's point was not that princes do follow the social contract, but that they ought to.

The delegates to the Constitutional Convention generally believed in the theory of the social contract, but by 1787 the thinkers among them had worked out a different version of it. The American view was that since all power originated in the people, they should *impose* the social contract on their rulers. That is, the people delegated certain powers to their government to do necessary tasks like defending the country from attack or making trade agreements with other nations. However, the final power remained with the people; they could take any or all of it back if they wished.

This theory of the social contract led to something else—the concept of a written constitution. Before the American example, European countries did not have written constitutions. In most cases kings and queens ruled by force.

England, however, was somewhat different. Over several centuries it had developed an "unwritten constitution." Even to this day the English constitution has not been written out the way the American one is. It is instead embodied in a host of royal proclamations, laws, court rulings, and traditions that set out the rights and duties of the rulers and the ruled.

From the days of the earliest settlements, Americans believed that it was best to "get it in writing," as the saying goes. The colonies all had written charters given them by the British government, and by 1787 eleven of the thirteen states had written constitutions. (Connecticut and Rhode Island just transformed their old royal charters into "constitutions.") Thus, the idea of the written constitution, while rare elsewhere, was familiar to Americans.

Our Constitution, then, is a written contract by which the people delegate certain powers to the government. This new social contract was not just theoretical; it had some very concrete results. For one, if the Constitution was a delegation of powers to the government by the people, it would have to be ratified by the people—that is, approved by them. The delegates could not simply announce that here was the new constitution that everyone had to obey. As we shall see, the delegates were by no means sure the people would ratify the Constitution, and they very nearly didn't.

Further, according to the American idea of the social contract, the people could take back powers they had given to the government. To make this possible the Convention put into the Constitution systems for

VIRGINIA CHARTERS.

NUMBER I.

King JAMES I.'s LETTERS PATENT to Sir Thomas Gates, Sir George Somers, and others, for two several Colonies and Plantations, to be made in VIRGINIA, and other Parts and Territories of AMERICA. Dated April 10, 1606.

I. JAMES, by the grace of God, King of England, Scotland, France, and Ireland, Defender of the Faith, &c. Whereas our loving and well disposed subjects, Sir Thomas Gates, and Sir George Somers, Knights, Richard Hackluit, Clerk, Prebendary of Westminster, and Edward-Maria Wingfield, Thomas Hanham, and Ralegh Gilbert, Esqrs. William Parker and George Popham, Gentlemen, and divers others of our loving subjects, have been humble suitors unto us, that We would vouchsafe unto them and may in time bring the infidels and savages, living in those parts, to human civility, and to a settled and quiet government; Do, by these our letters patents, graciously accept of, and agree to, their humble and well intended desires.

IV. And do therefore, for Us, our heirs and successors, Grant and agree, that the said Sir Thomas Gates, Sir George Somers, Richard Hackluit, and Edward-Maria Wingfield, adventurers of and for our city of London, and all such others, as are, or

Americans, right from the start, always liked to "get it in writing." The original colonies all had written charters drawn up by British monarchs, merchants, or other authorities, which spelled out the rights and duties of the colonists. This is a portion of the charter given to the first settlers in Virginia.

amending it. The American people, acting through their state governments, can change their Constitution any way they want, usually with the approval of three-quarters of the states. The Constitution has at this writing been amended twenty-seven times, mostly to modify in small ways how government works or to extend rights to people who did not originally have them.

The Idea of Federalism

The term *federalism* can be confusing. We use it most commonly when we speak of the federal government, as opposed to state or city governments. But federalism as political scientists use it means something a little different. A federation is a group of people or institutions joined together for some useful purpose. For example, sometimes companies in the same business form a federation to deal with common problems—say, to lobby the Congress for legislation favorable to their industry. Such a federation cannot tell the member companies how to run their business; it exists only to do specific tasks assigned to it by the members.

Another well-known federation is the United Nations. It tries to do certain jobs, like settle wars or feed people in times of famine. But it cannot interfere in the internal affairs of its member nations. It cannot, for example, stop nations from abusing the rights of their own people.

The American government under the Articles of Confederation was such a federation, as the title makes clear. The states kept virtually all of their original powers; they remained sovereign. The national federation could ask the states to send money and men to General Washington, but it could not force them to do it, as Washington often discovered to his great disgust.

Perhaps more significantly, the confederation government could not *require* individual citizens to do anything at all. It could not tax anybody, could not draft anybody into the army, could not charge anybody with a crime, even treason. It was a collection of state governments, and it had to work through those governments to get things done.

The delegates to the Convention knew that the people back home still thought of themselves first as New Yorkers, South Carolinians, Rhode Islanders, Virginians, and that they would not permit their states to be simply washed away. Indeed, most of the delegates, except the most extreme nationalists, also believed that the states had to retain a good deal of power. In writing the Constitution, they deliberately left most governmental power in the states.

We can see this in the makeup of the Senate: The key point is that, as in a federation, all members are considered equal to each other, regardless of size or anything else. So the Senate, with each state having the same number of senators—two—reflects the idea of federalism.

A second element of federalism in the Constitution is found in Article

The United Nations is a federation of most of the world's nations. It is empowered to do certain jobs, like bringing about peace among warring nations or aiding starving people in times of famine. However, as a federation, it cannot interfere in the internal policies of the member states. It cannot, for example, force a member state to give freedom of speech or of the press to its people. The United States under the old Articles of Confederation was such a federation and could not interfere in the policies of the individual states. At the Constitutional Convention one of the big arguments was over just how "federated" the new government ought to be. As a result, the United States today is only partly a federation.

I, section 8, which lists the powers of Congress—the things it can make laws about. This list, or "enumeration," as the delegates called it, includes the powers to lay taxes, borrow money, make treaties with foreign nations, declare war, coin money, and many others.

The Constitution of the United States contains an "enumeration" which spells out many of the national government's powers. It allows the government to institute taxes, for example, a necessary evil which most people don't like.

The question of whether the Constitution ought to contain such a list was cause for much debate at the Convention. Some people thought the national government should be given a "general grant," to the effect that it could do whatever was necessary for the common good, or some such wording. James Madison's Virginia Plan had included such a general grant, which said that the Congress could "legislate in all cases to which the states are incompetent, or in which the harmony of the United States may be interrupted by the exercise of individual legislation."

This was a broad grant. Who was to say what the "harmony" of the United States was? Madison himself did not really like the idea of a general grant. He told the Convention that he had put it in only because he did not know how a list of powers—the enumeration—could be drawn up in a way that would give the national government enough power without giving it too much.

At first the delegates agreed to the general grant. But as time went on, they began to have misgivings. Among other things, they were afraid that the people back home would never ratify a constitution that did not clearly spell out the powers of a new government. In the end, they put in a rather lengthy enumeration specifying the sorts of things the national government could make laws about. But then a loophole through which the United States Congress could acquire other powers was tacked on at the end of the enumeration. Congress was allowed to do anything "necessary and proper" in order to carry out the powers actually listed.

After the Constitution went into effect, the Tenth Amendment was added, which said, "The powers not delegated to the United States by the Constitution, nor prohibited by it to the States, are reserved to the States respectively, or to the people," thus making it very clear that the states were to have authority over all matters not mentioned. Nevertheless, the loophole has been more important than the restriction since the very beginning of the United States under the Constitution. (For a discussion of how this came about, see the eighth book of this series, *The Jeffersonian Republicans*.)

This element of federalism in our government is unusual. Before 1787 most governments were national; lower units such as counties and towns had no powers of their own except what the national government allowed. Many nations still operate this way. In England, for example, the national government sets policy for all the country's schools, issues drivers' licenses, sets closing hours for restaurants and bars, and deals with many other matters that in the United States are taken care of by state and local authorities.

The Idea of Nationalism

But if there remained a strong streak of federalism in the hearts of Americans, the Convention had been called to cure an overdose of it. Many of the most vocal delegates, like Washington, Madison, Wilson, Alexander Hamilton of New York, and Charles Pinckney of South Carolina, wanted a truly strong national government, with relatively little power left to the states. Even those who wanted the states to retain a good deal of power—like Roger Sherman, Luther Martin, and Gunning Bedford, for example—recognized that they had come to Philadelphia to strengthen the hand of the national government.

To begin with, the fact that representation in the House was based on population promoted the national idea. Where votes in the Senate would reflect the opinions of a majority of the state governments, votes in the House would express the views of a majority of the whole people. Moreover, the new government could now act directly on individuals without having to go through state governments. It could tax individuals, arrest them, and try them in its courts. A person could move from state to state, but he or she would always be subject to national laws.

The principle of nationalism was not merely implied in the Constitution; it was set forth explicitly in what is known as the Supremacy Clause, Article VI of the Constitution, which says:

> This Constitution, and the Laws of the United States which shall be made in Pursuance thereof; and all Treaties made, or which shall be made, under the Authority of the United States, shall be the supreme Law of the land; and the Judges in every State shall be bound thereby, anything in the Constitution and Laws of any State to the contrary notwithstanding.

The Supremacy Clause is quite clear: States cannot pass laws against the laws of the national government. Even state constitutions are limited not just by the U.S. Constitution, but also by laws passed by Congress. The delegates saw that it had to be this way, for the national government would be of no use at all if the states could pass laws contrary to national ones.

Adding to the strength of Article VI was a requirement that not only members of Congress and officers of the national government, but legislators and officials of the *state governments* too, must swear to support the national Constitution—even over their own state constitutions.

A third expression of the national idea lies in Article I, section 10, which lists a good many things that the states *cannot* do, such as issue their own money, make treaties with foreign countries, fight wars unless invaded, lay import and export taxes without the consent of Congress,

The Constitution gives the national government power over foreign affairs—the power to declare war and negotiate treaties. This photo shows President Harry Truman (in the dark suit, center) meeting with Prime Minister Winston Churchill of England (left) and Premier Joseph Stalin of the USSR (right) during treaty negotiations after World War II.

and a few other matters. This list makes it clear that the national government alone will be in charge of certain affairs.

Finally, the Constitution says, "The judicial Power of the United States shall be vested in one supreme Court, and in such inferior Courts as the Congress may from time to time ordain and establish." This clause was fleshed out in Amendments Five through Nine, passed not long after the government was established, which set up certain rules for running the courts. Under the Articles of Confederation, the old government had no power to arrest or try anybody; it could only settle disputes between states. The new Constitution gave the national government the power to arrest and try individual people for breaking laws. This clause put teeth into federal law. If, for example, a state governor resisted some federal order, he could be arrested by the national government and jailed.

The American government is thus partly federal and partly not. This is what historians call the federal *ambiguity*—a term meaning not exactly clear-cut. The federal ambiguity has caused some people to insist that the states really are supposed to have the last word on most matters. This "states' rights" idea was widely promoted before the Civil War by southerners who did not want the national government meddling in such matters as slavery. These people felt that the states were independent powers and could secede from the union if they wished. In fact, the states' rights position has been put forward at different times by different regions: New Englanders during the War of 1812; southerners from the 1830s through the 1860s and again in the 1950s. But events have worked against the states' rights position, and over two centuries the central government has come to dominate the state governments in most matters.

Nonetheless, there are some areas where it cannot rule. The government in Washington has no responsibility for education, for instance; nor for licensing doctors and lawyers; or regulating marriages, divorces, and other family matters. The states do have real power in these very close-to-home areas.

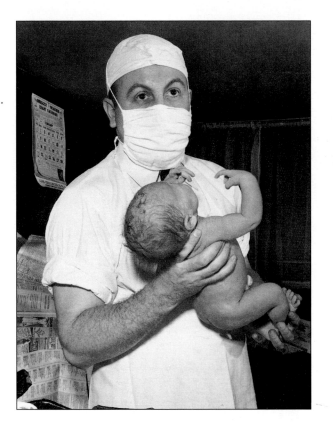

While the federal government does pass legislation regarding medical practices, for the most part rules and regulations for doctors and hospitals are under state and local control. Doctors are licensed to practice by states, not by the federal government.

The Idea of Separation of Powers

The Constitutional Convention and the document that grew out of it was fundamentally about power: How much should be given to whom? Most of the delegates were suspicious of power. For a hundred and fifty years the states had been struggling to keep the British government from having too much power over them, and only a few years before, they had been fighting a bloody war to get out from under the thumb of England. Most of these men knew history, as well. Through their studies they had come to believe that rulers were likely to abuse power if given the chance, and they were determined to see that the new government, did not get that chance. James Madison, in a famous statement, said:

Federal courts handle certain kinds of cases, especially ones where problems cross state lines. But most of the laws that Americans ordinarily deal with are state and local laws, and are handled by state and local courts.

> If men were angels, no government would be necessary.... In framing a government which is to be administered by men over men, the great difficulty lies in this: You must first oblige the government to control the governed; and in the next place oblige it to control itself.

Surprisingly, the idea of the separation of powers was not prominent in the minds of delegates when the Convention began. They came to Philadelphia believing that the best protection against a tyrant like George III would be a strong legislature, and at first they were thinking of an executive—the president—who would be the servant of the legislature, somebody who was just there to put into effect the laws passed by Congress.

Nonetheless, through the Confederation Era of the 1780s, the delegates had seen unruly state legislatures caught up in the passions of the moment, passing all those stay and tender laws put through by farmers twisting and turning under their debts. While the men at the Convention were certain that they wanted a weak executive, they also wanted some way of preventing Congress from hastily passing misguided laws in response to a sudden outcry from the people over some temporary change in the wind.

Long fearful of the power of English kings and their governors in the American colonies, the Founders began by planning for a weak executive. But as the idea of the separation of powers grew, they strengthened the presidency so the president could effectively balance the Congress. Today the occupant of the White House is indeed powerful, but is in turn checked by Congress.

But as we have seen, the Constitutional Convention was a learning process; as the debates went on, the concept of the separation of powers began to creep forward. Separation of powers had been suggested by a number of philosophers, including the famous John Locke, whose ideas kept cropping up at the Convention. However, it was best known to the delegates as stated by the French thinker Montesquieu. He pointed out that

> When the legislative and executive powers are united in the same person, or the same body of magistry, there can be no liberty; because apprehension may arise lest the same monarch or senate should *enact* tyrannical laws, to *execute* them in a tyrannical manner.

This is to say, if one person, such as a king, or one government body, like the English Parliament, could write laws and then arrest anyone who broke them, they could write laws aimed at, let us say, one religious group and then jail its members for worshiping as they liked. And, according to Montesquieu, it would be even worse if the same body also had the power to judge those who were arrested, for it could now find those worshippers guilty and put them away in prison for a long time.

The idea of the separation of powers really emerged when the delegates began arguing over what sort of president the new government should have. All kinds of ideas, many of them sounding strange to us today, were put forth. Some people wanted the executive to be a committee of three people. Some said he should be elected by Congress to do only what it told him to do. Others were afraid the president would hand out good jobs to the friends of legislators in order to get the legislators on his side, as George III and many colonial governors had done. The delegates wanted Congress, not the president, to appoint important government officials such as ambassadors and the Secretary of the Treasury.

But as the idea of the separation of powers grew more and more in the minds of the delegates, the powers of the president were step-by-step increased. The delegates saw that here was the way to keep Congress from rushing bad laws through in response to sudden outbursts from the people.

One delegate who played a major role in the shaping of our presidency was James Wilson of Pennsylvania. A brilliant man, he had grown

The Founding Fathers originally felt that the legislature ought to have the basic powers in the new government. As the convention went on, they came more and more to see the value in the idea of separation of powers, in which various branches of government, and even outside institutions like states, would check and balance each other. The Congress, shown here, thus became one of three theoretically equal branches of government.

up in Scotland, the son of a poor farmer, gone to a university there, and had emigrated to America as a young man. He quickly rose to prominence, because of his quick mind. Unhappily, Wilson got himself involved in speculating in western land. This was not unusual: Washington had also speculated in these lands. But Wilson's gambles turned out badly. Later on, when the new government was in place and Wilson was sitting on the Supreme Court, he had to flee from sheriffs pursuing him because of his debts. He died not long after in poverty and misery.

But that came later. At the Convention he was recognized as one of the smartest men there, and was very influential. Like Madison, Wilson wanted to build the new government on the people rather than on the states. But unlike anybody else there, he wanted to have the president as well as the Congress chosen by the people. All the other delegates assumed that the president would be picked by Congress or by state legislatures in some fashion. Among other problems, they did not see how the people could elect a president. There were in those days no political parties, no Democrats and Republicans, to nominate candidates for president, as they do today. If the people were to choose, they would surely vote for a thousand different candidates.

Challenged, Wilson came up with the idea of what we now know as our electoral college. The country would be divided into districts. The people from each district would choose an elector, and the electors would get together and choose a president.

The delegates were at first leery of Wilson's idea—it was very unusual. But now that the delegates had come to believe in the separation of powers, in which each arm of government would check and balance the other ones, they saw the advantages of a president who was independent of Congress, who could act as a check on it. And they swung around to Wilson's idea.

We still elect our presidents through the electoral college system. Each state is assigned a number of electoral votes according to population.

Under the Constitution each state government can decide for itself how its electors are chosen. But as it works today the candidate who gets the most popular votes in each state gets that state's electoral votes. Some historians have suggested that we ought to do away with the electoral college system, by which it is mathematically possible for the presidential candidate with the most popular votes to lose in the electoral college. This happened in 1888 when Benjamin Harrison had almost a hundred thousand fewer votes than Grover Cleveland but won in the electoral college.

The electoral college system unfortunately can sometimes work out so that the presidential candidate with the most votes comes in second in electoral votes. This can happen when a candidate loses by a lot of votes in some states, and wins by only a few votes in enough states to give him a majority of electoral votes. Benjamin Harrison (left) won in the electoral college even though Grover Cleveland (right) had the larger number of popular votes. Some political scientists believe that the system ought to be changed before this happens again.

Most of the debate over the presidency came toward the end of the Convention. By now the delegates were sure they wanted a president who could "check and balance" the Congress, and they gave him the power to veto its laws. But they did not want an executive who could dominate the legislature completely, so they gave Congress the power to override a presidential veto by a two-thirds majority in each house. The Congress could also impeach and remove the president from office, but it could not do it just because it didn't like the president's policies. The president could be impeached only for "Treason, Bribery, and other high Crimes and Misdemeanors." The president was to run foreign policy, make treaties, and appoint ambassadors, judges, and other officials, but only with the "advice and consent" of the Senate. And so it went: Every power given to one branch of government was checked or balanced in some way by a power given to another branch.

In the end, the delegates got the balance about as right as possible. At some times the presidents have been dominant, at other times the Congress, but rarely has one branch been able simply to ignore the wishes of the other.

Indeed, if anything, the opposite is more likely to be the case: The branches are so well balanced that the government sometimes seems paralyzed, unable to move in any direction because a Congress wants one thing and a president another, especially when each is dominated by a different political party. Many other democracies have parliamentary systems modeled on the British one. In this scheme the prime minister is in effect elected by the majority party in the Parliament, so the executive (the prime minister) and the majority in the legislature are always of the same political party and support the same policies. It may be, however, that some moments of paralysis are a small price to pay for insurance against dominance by one branch.

Of course, there is a third branch to our government: the Supreme Court, along with the lower Federal courts. They act as a check on the other two branches: In the course of trying cases, the courts must interpret state and national laws, and if they find these laws in violation of the Constitution, they can declare them void.

Surprisingly, the Constitution itself does not give the Supreme Court and other Federal courts this power. So fearful of tyranny were the men at the Convention that they could not bring themselves to give any branch of government the final say. Yet obviously somebody had to be able to say whether a law violated the Constitution, otherwise Congress and the president together could pass any kind of law they liked. As soon as the new government was established, Senator Oliver Ellsworth, who had been a delegate from Connecticut, wrote the Judiciary Act of 1789. This act gave the Supreme Court the right to declare *state* laws unconsti-

The Founding Fathers had a lot of trouble deciding just exactly how the Supreme Court would fit into the system of checks and balances. Most of the Supreme Court's powers to declare laws unconstitutional were given to it later by the new government or simply assumed by the Court through its rulings.

tutional; and by implication it allowed the Supreme Court to declare Federal laws unconstitutional as well. Later Court decisions, particularly a famous case called *Marbury* v. *Madison,* made this the rule. (For a full discussion of this issue, readers can turn to the seventh book of this series, *Building a New Nation.*)

Nonetheless, it is doubtful that very many of the Founding Fathers would have given the Supreme Court the vast powers it has now. In recent decades the Supreme Court, not the Congress, has been deciding how state legislatures must be constituted, dealing with racial segregation, setting rules for abortion, and much else. Many people believe that the Supreme Court has grabbed too much power for itself. Others disagree; they say times have changed, bringing problems that the Founding Fathers could not have guessed at. Perhaps Congress should deal with more of them, but if it does not, somebody has to. It has fallen to the court to play that role.

CHAPTER VI

Ratification and the Bill of Rights

The foregoing discussion of the Constitutional Convention, lengthy as it has been, touched only the high spots. The delegates debated a great many other questions, such as what sort of defense force the United States should have and who should command it, how new states were to be admitted, and much else. But finally, on September 17, 1787, it was done. Not everybody was entirely pleased with the result. Madison himself was disappointed, and three delegates actually would not sign the new Constitution. Most of them felt, however, as Benjamin Franklin said in a closing speech, that while the Constitution was not perfect, it was certainly very good, and in any case, it was unlikely that a better one could be written. Most of the delegates went off to the City Tavern for a celebratory dinner in a very cheerful frame of mind.

Now the Constitution had to be ratified, that is, approved by the people. Conventions would be held in every state, at which the people's representatives would vote for or against the Constitution. It would go into effect when nine states had ratified.

Considering how much we value our Constitution today, it is startling to realize that in 1787 probably the majority of Americans were opposed

The City Tavern, the building at left, was one of the best-known inns in Philadelphia. It was a regular meeting place for delegates, many of whom stayed there that long, hot summer of 1787. The building at right is the Bank of Pennsylvania. It was built later.

to it. Like the delegates, they were fearful of giving too much power to anybody, particularly at the expense of their own states. They were especially bothered that the Constitution had in it no bill of rights. It was by no means a sure thing that the states would ratify.

However, opinion in favor of the new Constitution was strong in the small states. They saw that here was their best, and perhaps last, chance to protect themselves from the big states. Delaware and New Jersey ratified almost immediately; Connecticut in January; Maryland in April.

The three southernmost states also saw the need for a strong national government. As Washington put it, ". . . if a weak state with Indians on its back and Spaniards on its flank does not see the necessity of a general government, there must, I think, be wickedness or insanity in the way." Georgia saw the necessity and ratified in January, and South Carolina followed. North Carolina, worried about giving away too much of its power and the lack of a bill of rights, held out.

But the new government had to include the "Big Three" to succeed.

The battle in Pennsylvania was hard-fought, but the state ratified quickly. In Massachusetts the independent farmers in the western half of the state were suspicious of any kind of government. They had only a year before fought Shays' Rebellion against a government they believed was controlled by the rich and powerful men on the eastern seaboard. They were not eager to establish over them an even more powerful national government. However, Governor John Hancock was persuaded to support ratification. He was very popular in his state, and he tipped the balance. With Massachusetts, eight states had ratified.

The key was now Virginia. If it did not ratify, New York, which was tipping away, would probably not ratify either, in which case the new nation might not be formed. In Virginia the battle against the Constitution was led by Patrick Henry, the most famous speaker of the day. He harangued the delegates for hours at a time. But Madison and others in favor kept boring back with carefully thought-out arguments,

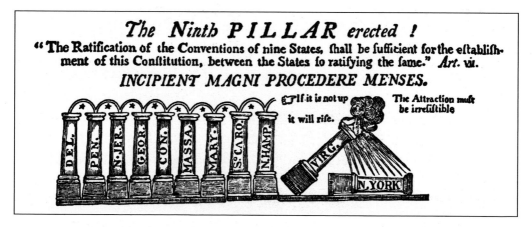

New York was undecided about ratifying the Constitution, and if Virginia had failed to ratify, New York would probably have stayed out. With these two states missing, the new nation might not have come into being. But as this cartoon of the day shows, New York was bound to be pulled in by Virginia's ratification.

and in a close vote Virginia ratified on June 25. New Hampshire had actually ratified four days earlier, although that had not been known in Virginia. The opponents now saw that the battle was over, and New York quickly ratified. North Carolina and Rhode Island held out until the new government wrote a bill of rights, and then they too joined the Union.

Why, considering that so many Americans had opposed the Constitution at first, was it ratified with speed, remarkable for a day when transportation and communication were slow and difficult? One reason was that the people leading the fight for the Constitution, such as Madison, Hamilton, Pinckney, Sherman, Wilson, and others, had spent a summer debating the document. They knew thoroughly every argument for and against each point in it. They were aided by a series of pamphlets published during the ratification fight, called the *Federalist Papers*, written by Madison, Alexander Hamilton, and John Jay of New York, who was not at the Convention. These papers are among the most important documents in American history, for they are filled with ideas and explanations about the Constitution. They remain the classic discussion of the American Constitution and continue to influence political thinkers around the world.

Another reason the Constitution was ratified so quickly—although only after sometimes bitter debate—is that there was no single set of ideas put forward in some "Antifederalist Papers" that could gain the support of some important men across all the states. Indeed, the antifederalists were able to organize effective political movements in only a few states.

But perhaps the main reason the Constitution was ratified was that the most influential political leaders saw no alternative. The nation could not go back to the old system under the Articles of Confederation. The Antifederalists could come up with no better suggestion than to hold another convention to revise the plan. But it was unrealistic to believe that another convention could think up anything that was likely to get wider agreement than the proposed draft—or agreement on anything at all, for that matter. The Constitution written in that steamy Philadelphia heat during the summer of 1787 was the only choice.

The Bill of Rights

It had become obvious to everyone long before ratification was complete that a bill of rights had to be added. The American people insisted upon it. They were very familiar with the idea of a bill of rights. Over many centuries the English people, through much struggle, had gathered certain rights to themselves, such as the right to a trial by jury, the right not to have their property seized by the government for no reason, and others. In 1689 some of these traditional rights were written down in England as a Bill of Rights.

Americans had fought the British in a long, hard war, mainly to keep or gain certain rights. After the victory, when the former colonies became little—or not so little—independent nations, they wrote constitutions for themselves, and almost always included bills of rights, usually modeled on that of Virginia written by George Mason in 1776, which in turn was modeled at least in part on the English Bill of Rights. Such fences against tyranny were critically important to Americans. Why, then, did the Convention fail to put one in?

In the first place, a bill of rights does not *give* us anything. It merely lists some of the natural rights we were born with. These rights—and many more not listed—are ours just because we exist. But there were specific reasons why a bill was not included in the original Constitution.

Different delegates had different reasons. One southern delegate said that bills of rights generally began with some statement to the effect that "all men are created free and equal." Such a statement, he went on, would be received "with very bad grace when a large part of our property consist in men who are actually born slaves."

A second objection to a bill of rights came from Roger Sherman. He said that state bills of rights still stood; a national one was unnecessary and might conflict with the state bills. Indeed, the delegates generally agreed that the state bills would provide adequate protection.

Alexander Hamilton had yet another view: A list of rights might imply that rights not on the list did not exist. In fact, we have many more rights than are listed anywhere. To list just a few, Hamilton thought, was risky.

The American people disagreed, and almost as soon as the new government was in place, the Bill of Rights was added. Today, our Bill of Rights is the part of the Constitution Americans know best. Indeed, it seems to many people to be the heart of the Constitution, with its guarantees of free speech, freedom of religion, trial by jury, a free press. And the Ninth Amendment declares that just because the Bill of Rights lists a few rights, that doesn't mean we don't have a lot of others.

One of our most important rights is the right to free speech, and in particular the right to criticize government itself. Politics could hardly exist if people were not allowed to tell voters how they could do things better than the government in office.

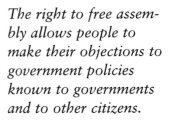

The right to free assembly allows people to make their objections to government policies known to governments and to other citizens.

Unfortunately, we do not always understand the Bill of Rights as well as we might. Many people seem to think that it guarantees us the right to do almost anything we want. That is not the case; there are limits. For example, the right to free speech does not give us the right to say slanderous things about others, to cry fire in a crowded theater as a joke, or to discuss military secrets with our friends. The right to peaceable assembly does not permit us to gather a crowd of demonstrators in the middle of a busy street. As interpreted by the Supreme Court, the rights of individuals must be balanced against the needs of the society as a whole.

Under our Constitution, government is always such a balancing act. How can freedom of the press be balanced against the wish of many parents not to have their children exposed to excessive violence in the media? How can a person's right to do what he wants with his property, like a factory or a forest, be balanced against controlling pollution from

Balancing the rights of one individual against another's, or against the general welfare, is often difficult. In fact, one of the most important tasks of government is to make such decisions. For example, should the government be able to require the owners of a mill to stop polluting the air, when antipollution devices will cost the owners money?

The society built under the Constitution has allowed Americans not only to keep their freedoms but to become the most prosperous nation on earth. When in most places automobiles were a luxury for the rich, American workers could own them, as the automobiles of coal miners near Pottsville, Pennsylvania, make clear.

a smokestack or saving rare species of trees? There are always troublesome questions to deal with.

Yet the surprising thing is that almost from the moment the new government was in place, Americans began to see how good the new Constitution was. It seemed to them that in setting up their own government for themselves, they had done a remarkable thing. And they had.

EPILOGUE

The American Constitution, as Prime Minister William Gladstone said, is indeed a "remarkable work." It has over the years been amended by the people and interpreted by the Supreme Court, but this has been mainly to guarantee rights to blacks, women, and others who had been left out, and to fine-tune governmental machinery. Only the Fourteenth Amendment has made a fundamental difference in our federal system, by restricting the states in many areas. At bottom, the Constitution stands pretty much as originally written. Under it, the nation has not merely flourished, but has become the most prosperous and innovative nation on earth, one that other nations have increasingly looked to for leadership. The United States has also been, for more than two hundred years, politically more free than other nations.

Why has the Constitution worked so well? One reason is that many of the men who wrote it had taken the trouble to learn their history and to study other forms of government such as the old Greek and Roman systems and, of course, the British government they had lived under for most of their lives. They knew political theory.

But as Charles Pinckney of South Carolina said very early in the

Convention, America was a new and different place. The delegates could not look to other models but must create something new and different. Most of the delegates were practical politicians. However much theory they knew, they also knew the ways of the world, and they understood that the new government would not work if the interests of any significant group were not taken into account. The big and small states, the North and the South, the farmers and the traders—all had to be protected from one another. And as we have seen, the delegates carefully compromised these various interests.

Beyond this, the delegates were realistic about human nature. As one historian has said, "They shared a profound mistrust of man's capacity to use power wisely and well. They believed self-interest to be the dominant motive of political behavior." People in government might behave wisely and well; but it would be foolish to count on it. There were always selfish and grasping people who would take advantage of loopholes; the delegates worked hard to see that there were no such loopholes. In particular, they put in that system of checks and balances so the self-interest of one branch of government would prevent the self-interest of another branch from overreaching. The American government works even when it has been in the hands of fools, knaves, and ignoramuses, as has sometimes happened.

This does not mean that the Founders got everything right. As we have seen, the northern states could probably have driven a harder bargain with the southern ones over the slave trade. As we have also seen, some people think the Supreme Court has been left to rule on matters that Congress should have tackled. Finally, the Founders never really came to terms with the Federal ambiguity. Why, for example, should some roads be built by towns, some by counties, some by states, some by the Federal government? Why are pilots licensed by the U.S. government, but truck drivers by the states?

The ambiguities of the Constitution, however, are one of its saving characteristics. Because many of the sections of the Constitution are open to various interpretations—often conflicting ones—it has been possible to adapt it to conditions that have undergone radical change over the generations since our eighteenth-century forebears wrote it. This flexibility, indeed, is what gives it its strength and durability.

The Founders, then, got most of it right. In particular, they managed to give the national government enough power to get things done without infringing on people's basic liberties. The United States for the most part works effectively, yet the rights of the people are safeguarded. That of itself is little short of a miracle.

At the close of the Convention, when the new Constitution had been approved, Benjamin Franklin made a short speech, saying that all through the Convention he had been looking at the sun on the back of George Washington's chair, trying to decide if it were rising or setting. "But now at length I have the happiness to know that is a rising and not a setting sun." He was right.

BIBLIOGRAPHY

For Students

Faber, Doris, and Harold Faber. *The Birth of a Nation: The Early Years of the United States*. New York: Atheneum, 1989.

Johnson, Linda Carlson. *Our Constitution*. Brookfield, Conn.: Millbrook Press, 1992.

Meltzer, Milton, ed. *The American Revolutionaries: A History in Their Own Words, 1750–1800*. New York: T.Y. Crowell, 1987.

Meltzer, Milton. *The Bill of Rights: How We Got It and What It Means*. New York: T.Y. Crowell, 1990.

For Teachers

Banning, Lance. *The Sacred Fire of Liberty: James Madison and the Founding of the Federal Republic*. Ithaca, N.Y.: Cornell University Press, 1995.

Collier, Christopher, and James Lincoln Collier. *Decision in Philadelphia: The Constitutional Convention of 1787*. New York: Random House, 1986.

Miller, William Lee. *The Business of May Next: James Madison and the Founding*. Charlottesville, Va.: University Press of Virginia, 1992.

Morris, Richard B. *The Forging of the Union, 1781–1789*. New York: HarperCollins, 1988.

Rutland, Robert Allen. *The Birth of the Bill of Rights, 1776–1791*. Rev. ed. Chapel Hill: University of North Carolina Press, 1982.

Wood, Gordon S. *The Creation of the American Republic, 1776–1787*. Chapel Hill: University of North Carolina Press, 1969.

INDEX

Note: Page numbers for illustrations are in **boldface**.

JAMES LINCOLN COLLIER is the author of a number of books both for adults and for young people, including the social history *The Rise of Selfishness in America*. He is also noted for his biographies and historical studies in the field of jazz. Together with his brother, Christopher Collier, he has written a series of award-winning historical novels for children widely used in schools, including the Newbery Honor classic, *My Brother Sam Is Dead*. A graduate of Hamilton College, he lives with his wife in New York City.

CHRISTOPHER COLLIER grew up in Fairfield County, Connecticut and attended public schools there. He graduated from Clark University in Worcester, Massachusetts and earned M.A. and Ph.D. degrees at Columbia University in New York City. After service in the Army and teaching in secondary schools for several years, Mr. Collier began teaching college in 1961. He is now Professor of History at the University of Connecticut and Connecticut State Historian. Mr. Collier has published many scholarly and popular books and articles about Connecticut and American history. With his brother, James, he is the author of nine historical novels for young adults, the best known of which is *My Brother Sam Is Dead*. He lives with his wife Bonnie, a librarian, in Orange, Connecticut.